T0036185

TO:

FROM:

FINISH STRONG

Amazing Stories of Courage and Inspiration

DAN GREEN

Copyright © 2008, 2020 by Dan Green
Cover and internal design © 2020 by Sourcebooks
Cover design by Ploy Siripant

Sourcebooks, Simple Truths, and the colophon are registered trademarks of Sourcebooks.

All rights reserved. No part of this book may be reproduced in any form or by any electronic or mechanical means including information storage and retrieval systems—except in the case of brief quotations embodied in critical articles or reviews—without permission in writing from its publisher, Sourcebooks.

This publication is designed to provide accurate and authoritative information in regard to the subject matter covered. It is sold with the understanding that the publisher is not engaged in rendering legal, accounting, or other professional service. If legal advice or other expert assistance is required, the services of a competent professional person should be sought.—*From a Declaration of Principles Jointly Adopted by a Committee of the American Bar Association and a Committee of Publishers and Associations*

All brand names and product names used in this book are trademarks, registered trademarks, or trade names of their respective holders. Sourcebooks is not associated with any product or vendor in this book.

Photo Credits
Internal images © page x, Comstock/Getty Images; page xiii, boonchai wedmakawand/Getty Images; page 4, Thomas Barwick/Getty Images; page 9, Yellow Dog Productions/Getty Images; page 12, Chinnapong/Getty Images; page 20-21, David Merron Photography/Getty Images; page 30, aylinstock/Getty Images; page 35, Gary Kellner/Getty Images; page 47, Cecilie_Arcurs/Getty Images; page 51, Nora Carol Photography/Getty Images; page 52, mevans/Getty Images; page 58, Stígur Már Karlsson/Heimsmyndir/Getty Images; page 59, LWA/Getty Images; page 60, the_burtons/Getty Images; page 64, Camerique/ClassicStock/Getty Images; page 71, Mārtiņš Zemlickis/Unsplash; page 73, Digital Light Source/Getty Images; page 74, The Stanley Weston Archive/Getty Images; page 79, MGSmith/Getty Images; page 85, Augustas Cetkauskas/Getty Images; page 88, Keystone-France/Getty Images; page 91, Bibica/Getty Images; page 96, South_agency/Getty Images; page 100, Jigsawstocker/Freepik page 103, mihailomilovanovic/Getty Images; page 104, EyesWideOpen/Getty Images; page 106, jacobeukman/Getty Images;
Internal image on page 73 provided by Unsplash, licensed under CC0 Creative Commons and released by the author for use.

Published by Simple Truths, an imprint of Sourcebooks
P.O. Box 4410, Naperville, Illinois 60567-4410
(630) 961-3900
sourcebooks.com

Originally published as *Finish Strong* in 2008 in the United States of America by Simple Truths, an imprint of Sourcebooks. This edition issued based on the hardcover edition published in 2008 in the United States of America by Simple Truths, an imprint of Sourcebooks.

Printed and bound in China.
OGP 10 9 8 7 6 5 4 3 2 1

To my daughters Laikin and Raigin.

Thank you for your strength and Finish Strong spirit.

CONTENTS

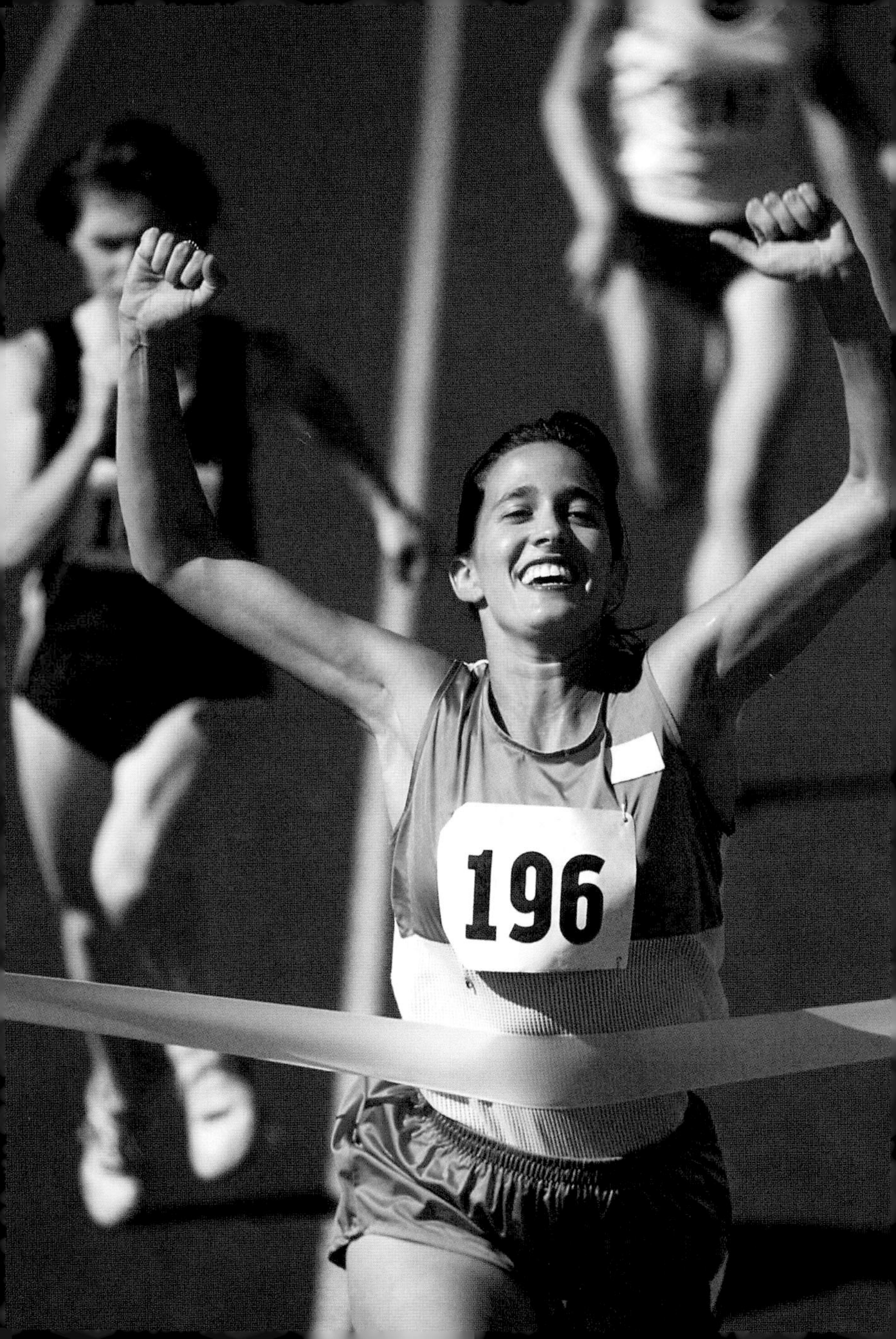
196

INTRODUCTION

Finish Strong. To me, these two words more clearly define a call to action than any other two words in the English language. I challenge you to find two words that more absolutely define a performance objective. The words *Finish Strong* are pervasively used in our culture, and they are a perfect example of how the whole is greater than the sum of the parts. **When you combine** *finish* **with** *strong,* **you create a powerful platform for action.** It's not uncommon for these words to flow from the mouths of athletes as they describe their goals in pre- and post-event interviews. The media uses these words to describe the performance of everything from the stock market to stock car racing. And for as long as man has documented history, the spirit of these words has existed.

> **Believe and act as if it were impossible to fail.**
>
> **—Charles F. Kettering**

The phrase *Finish Strong* has become a driving force in my life. For more than ten years, they have been my personal mantra for achieving excellence in life, sport, and business. I have personally embraced the Finish Strong mindset in all aspects of my life. And when faced with a challenge or adversity, I remind myself, regardless of what came before or what has yet to come, what matters most right now is how I choose to respond to the challenge before me. Will I lie down or will I fight? The choice is mine, and I choose to Finish Strong.

From this attitude, I have created a personal level of accountability for everything I do. I don't always get the result I want, but when I have leaned on my commit-ment, I always felt a greater sense of accomplishment and satisfaction knowing that I gave it all I had.

The purpose of this book is to introduce you to the Finish Strong attitude and hope that you will embrace it. The stories I've chosen are timeless and amazing examples of people who exemplify the Finish Strong spirit in sport, business, and life. Therefore, my wish for you is to always Finish Strong!

COURAGE

Most of us have far more courage than
we ever dreamed we possessed.

—Dale Carnegie

Have the courage to live.
Anyone can die.

—Robert Cody

Courage is almost a contradiction in
terms. It means a strong desire to live
taking the form of a readiness to die.

—G. K. Chesterton

FEAR IS IN THE EYE OF THE BEHOLDER

It was a picture-perfect day for surfing at Tunnels Beach, Kauai. A thirteen-year-old surfing prodigy had just finished riding a twenty foot wave and was lying face down on her surf board, dangling her arms in the cool morning water. Preparing to paddle out to catch another wave, her thoughts of becoming a professional surfer shifted in an instant. Without warning, she felt a tug on her left arm, and in a split second, she realized that she'd been attacked by a shark.

As she struggled to gain her composure, she realized something even more horrifying: the fourteen-foot tiger shark had bitten clean through her board, taking her left arm in a single bite. At that moment in time, survival, not surfing, became a priority.

Bethany Hamilton learned to surf at the age of four. When she was eight, she entered her first contest and won both events she competed in. At the age of ten, she placed first in the girls under eleven, first in the girls under fifteen, and second in the boys under twelve divisions at the Volcom Pufferfish contest. She was determined to become a professional surfer and was certainly on track to make it happen. Then, in one violently swift moment on that fall day in 2003, it seemed her dreams would be shattered.

However, Bethany was born with the heart of a lion and the competitive spirit of a thoroughbred. She was determined to return to the water to surf. Leaning on support from her friends, her family, and her faith in God, Bethany recovered rapidly, and within ten weeks of the attack, she was surfing again. Convinced she could overcome her physical challenge, she worked hard to learn to surf despite her disability. But she also had to overcome the psychological fear of another attack. Bethany faced her fears by singing and praying when she was out on the water.

Incredible as it seems, less than a year after her attack, Bethany returned to competition, taking fifth place at the National Surfing Championships and first place at the first event for the Hawaii Conference of the National Scholastic Surfing Association. She was recognized by ESPN in 2004 and received an ESPY award for Best Comeback Athlete of the year.

Bethany's ability to overcome her physical and mental challenges puts her in an elite class of achievers. She chose to Finish Strong.

Her unique ability to confront her fears, embrace them, and then continue moving forward in the direction of her goals is the perfect definition of courage.

WHAT'S IN A NAME?

John Baker was too short and slight to be a runner for his high school track team. But John loved to run, and he wanted to make the team. His best friend, John Haaland, was a tall and promising runner and heavily recruited by the Manzano High School track coach, but he wanted nothing to do with the sport. John Baker convinced the track coach to let him join the team under the premise that his best friend would follow. The coach agreed, and John Baker became a runner.

The team's first meet was a 1.7-mile cross-country race through the foothills of Albuquerque. The reigning state champion, Lloyd Goff, was running, and all eyes were on him. The race began, and the pack of runners led by Goff disappeared behind the hill. The spectators waited. A minute passed, then two and three. Then the silhouette of a single runner appeared. The crowd assumed it was one of the favorites. But to everyone's amazement, it was John Baker leading the way to the finish line. In his first meet, he blew away the field and set a new meet record.

When asked what happened behind the hill, John explained that at the halfway point of the run, he was struggling hard. He asked himself a question:

Am I doing my best?

Still unsure if he truly was giving his best effort, he fixed his eyes on the back of the runner in front of him. *One at a time*, he thought. His entire focus was on one thing—passing the runner in front of him.

He committed to himself that nothing would distract him—fatigue, pain, nothing. One by one, he caught up to and passed each runner in front of him until there was no one else to pass.

As the season progressed, John proved that first

race was not a fluke. Once the race began, the fun-loving, unassuming teenager became a fierce and relentless competitor who refused to lose. By the end of his junior year, he had broken six meet records and was largely regarded as the best miler in the state. In his senior year, he ran the entire track and cross-country season undefeated, winning the state championship in both events.

The future certainly looked bright for the seventeen-year-old.

John entered the University of New Mexico in 1962 and took his training to the next level by running over ten miles a day. In the spring of 1965, he and his team faced the most feared team in track—the University of Southern California Trojans. There was little doubt that the mile belonged to the Trojans. During the race, John led for the first lap, then purposely slipped back to fourth. At the far turn of the third lap, he collided with another runner vying for position. John stumbled and struggled to stay on his feet, losing valuable time. With just under 330 yards to go, he dug deep, and living up to his reputation, he blew past the leaders to take the victory by three seconds.

Yes, the future looked even brighter for John Baker. After graduating college, he set his sights on the 1972 Olympics. To have time to train and also make a living, he took a coaching position at Aspen Elementary in Albuquerque, where he had the opportunity to work with kids, something he always wanted to do.

Within a few months, Coach Baker became known as the coach who cared. He invested a great deal of time and energy into working with his students as individuals. He was not a critical coach but only demanded what he demanded of himself: that each child give their best effort. The kids responded and loved learning from Coach Baker.

In May 1969, just before his twenty-fifth birthday, John noticed that he was tiring prematurely during his workouts. Two weeks later, he developed chest pains, and one morning, he woke with a painfully

swollen groin. He went to see his doctor, and they discovered that John had an advanced form of testicular cancer. The only chance he had was to undergo surgery. The operation confirmed the worst case: his cancer had spread. His doctor believed that he had at best six months to live. A second operation would be required.

I can't even begin to imagine the devastation that John Baker must have felt.

How easy it would have been to lie down, quit, and feel sorry for himself. In fact, shortly before the second operation, John drove to the mountains and prepared to end his life. He did not want to put his family through the pain. Just before he thought of driving off the cliff, he recalled the faces of the children at Aspen and wondered if they would think that this was the best that Coach Baker could do. This was not the legacy he wanted to leave behind.

At that moment, he decided to rededicate his life to the kids and continue striving to give his best effort. He was not a quitter. He drove home determined to give his best effort for the rest of his life.

In September, after extensive surgery and a summer of treatments, John returned to Aspen where he added a unique program to include children with disabilities within the sports program. He appointed kids as "Coach's Time Keeper" or "Chief Equipment Supervisor." Everyone who wanted to be was included. By Thanksgiving, letters from parents were arriving daily at Aspen Elementary in praise of Coach Baker. He created a special award for any child he thought deserved recognition. He used his own trophies as awards, carefully polishing off his own name. He purchased special fabric with his own money, and at night, he would cut blue ribbons to give as awards.

John refused to take medication to help with his pain because he was afraid of how it would impair his ability to work with the kids. In early 1970, he was asked to help coach a small Albuquerque track club for girls— the Duke City Dashers. By that summer, the Dashers were a team to contend with. John boldly predicted that they would make it to the Amateur Athletic Union (AAU) finals.

By now, John's condition was complicated by chemotherapy treatments. He could not keep any food down, his health rapidly deteriorated, and he struggled to make it to his practices. One October at practice, a girl ran up to Coach Baker and shouted, "Coach, your prediction came true. We're going to the

AAU championship next month." John was elated and wished for one remaining hope—to live long enough to go along. Unfortunately, it was not to be. A few weeks later, John clutched his abdomen and collapsed. He would not be able to make the trip. Then, at the age of twenty-six, on Thanksgiving Day in 1970, John Baker passed away, eighteen months after his first visit to the doctor. He had beaten the odds by twelve months. Two days later, the Duke City Dashers won the AAU championship in St. Louis—"for Coach Baker."

As it stands, that would have been the end of the story. Except a few days after his funeral, the children at Aspen Elementary began calling their school "John Baker School," and others rapidly adopted this change. A movement began to make the new name official. The Aspen principal referred the matter to the Albuquerque school board.

In the spring of 1971, 520 families in the Aspen district voted on the matter. There were 520 votes for the name change and none against. That May, at a ceremony attended by hundreds of John's friends, family, and students, Aspen Elementary officially became John Baker Elementary.

Today, John Baker Elementary stands as a testament to a courageous young man who believed in giving his best effort to the very end. His legacy continues through the dedicated efforts of the John Baker Foundation. The following poem is used with the permission of his foundation and was written by John five years before he was diagnosed with cancer:

Many thoughts race through my mind

As I step up to the starting line.

Butterflies thru my stomach fly

And as I free that last deep sigh,

I feel that death is drawing near,

But the end of the race I do not fear.

For when the string comes across
   my breast,

I know it's time for eternal rest.

The gun goes off, the race is run,

And only God knows if I've won.

My family and friends and many more

Can't understand what it was for.

But this "Race To Death" is a final test,

And I'm not afraid, for I've done my best.

—John Baker

FAITH

Faith is believing what
you know ain't so.

—Mark Twain

The only thing that stands between
a person and what they want
in life is the will to try it and the
faith to believe it possible.

—Rich Devos

All things are possible to him
who believes.

—Mark 9:23

AN EXPEDITION IN FAITH

On August 1, 1914, Sir Ernest Shackleton set sail with a crew of twenty-eight on an expedition to the Antarctic. The goal of their expedition was to cross the Antarctic on foot—something never done before. Shackleton was a successful and highly respected explorer known for his faith, determination, and conviction, and was knighted for a prior successful expedition to Antarctica in 1907–1909.

To recruit his crew of twenty-eight, he took applications from five thousand men. Many believe that he placed the following ad in a London newspaper to attract the applicants. While there is no evidence that this ad actually ran, it does quite appropriately frame the expectations that Shackleton had for the type of men he was looking for.

> **MEN WANTED:** For hazardous journey. Small wages, bitter cold, long months of complete darkness, constant danger, safe return doubtful. Honor and recognition in case of success.

This expedition was going to be different from any other one Shackleton had led. Five months into the expedition, their ship, the *Endurance*, became stuck in the heavy ice floes near Antarctica. This was not an uncommon occurrence, and Shackleton had the experience and confidence that the ice would eventually recede and free the ship. His focus was on the expedition, and he held fast to that course. However, the situation grew worse. Over the next three weeks, the ship became solidly frozen in the ice, and countless attempts to free it from the ice's grasp were futile. At the end of February 1915, the crew prepared the ship to become their camp for the remainder of winter.

The goal of the expedition had to change if they were to survive. Shackleton abandoned his primary goal and turned his focus toward saving his men and returning to England. This expedition became a rescue mission.

By October, eight months after being stuck, the pressure created by the ice finally took its toll on the *Endurance*. The ship began to be crushed and started to sink, making it uninhabitable. The order to abandon ship was given, and the entire crew began to salvage as many supplies as they could. They took the sled dogs, food, gear, and three lifeboats and moved their camp to the ice floe adjacent to their sinking ship. The temperatures were brutal, reaching -15°F below on an average day. For the next five months, the expedition camped on the ice floe, surviving on what little food they had left. In April, the ice they were camped on began to break apart. Shackleton ordered the crew to take only essential supplies and board the lifeboats.

They fled the disintegrating ice floe and traveled seven days by sea to Elephant Island, an amazing feat in and of itself. Elephant Island was a barren place to be stranded, made up mostly of snow-covered rock, with temperatures reaching -20°F. For the next nine months, under Shackleton's leadership, the broken expedition remained loyal, optimistic, focused, and faithful to their leader's belief that they would survive. Ultimately, Shackleton knew that their survival depended upon his ability to get off the barren rock and return to the island of South Georgia, where they had replenished their supplies almost a year earlier. But the island was more than eight hundred miles away, across what was

regarded by sailors to be the most treacherous ocean seas in the world. Determined to save his crew, he modified one of the lifeboats by adding a deck and extra sail. Those changes would prepare the ship for the journey ahead. He set sail with five crew members to make the journey. The odds of making it were one in one hundred. Nautical scholars consider this journey by lifeboat to be one of the greatest nautical accomplishments in maritime history and is another story to be told. Fourteen days after sailing away from Elephant Island, Shackleton and his crew landed on South Georgia Island. As luck would have it, they landed on the wrong side of the island, twenty-two miles from the

whaling outpost. Another journey lay ahead. In order to reach the outpost, they would have to hike across the mountain ridge and glaciers that stood between them and the outpost. Against unsurmountable odds, after five days of walking through treacherous ice and snow, they reached the whaling outpost. However, because the seas were unnavigable (ironically, the very seas that the six men had just crossed in lifeboat) they were forced to wait four months before rescuing their mates on Elephant Island.

On August 30, 1916, after twenty-two months of being stranded on a barren rock in subzero temperatures, the crew of the *Endurance* was rescued. All twenty-eight crew members survived the ordeal, and most were quick to credit the strong faith of their leader, "the Boss" as they called him, as the catalyst in their survival. Without question, the adventures of the *Endurance* expedition represent some of the finest examples of refusing to quit, adjusting your goals, and choosing to Finish Strong!

IT AIN'T OVER TILL IT'S OVER

Paul Hamm had high expectations going into the 2004 Summer Olympics in Athens. He was the reigning men's gymnastics world champion—the first U.S. man to win a world all-around title. No American had ever won the all-around gold medal in men's gymnastics, and Paul was expected to change that. To that point, the only U.S. gymnast to medal in the men's all-around competition was Peter Vidmar in the 1984 Olympics. Paul Hamm seemed destined to at least join Vidmar by standing on the podium with one of the three medals.

Paul started strong in the first three events and held the lead in the all-around by .038 points. Then disaster struck. During his vault performance, he under-rotated and missed his landing, causing him to sit down and nearly fall off the platform. His score reflected the cardinal sin of gymnastics, and after the vault competition was over, Paul found himself in twelfth place. I remember watching the telecast and seeing him sitting on the sidelines with a pale look on his face. It was pretty clear by his reaction that at that point in time, he believed he had blown his chance of making history.

But this is where Paul Hamm demonstrated the difference between mediocrity and greatness. He decided at that moment to put his fall behind him and move forward, giving his best effort to Finish Strong. His next event was coming up, and he was first up. He pulled off a great routine on the parallel bars and nailed his dismount. During the next rotation, a few of the competitors in the sixth to eleventh places struggled. His great performance on the parallel bars coupled with the struggles of his competitors helped to move Paul into fourth place in the all-around with his last and strongest event left to play out—the high bar.

Paul was determined to take advantage of this positive turn of events and make sure that he at least won the bronze medal. He was a master of the high bar, and he scripted a highly technical routine in order to have a shot at earning the most points possible. The die was cast, as the other competitors had finished their routines. Paul was the last to go. As I sat and watched the broadcast, I could see him pour his heart into his routine. You could feel his energy, focus, and determination. When he nailed his dismount, it was electrifying, and even before his score was revealed, you could see on Paul's face that in his own mind, he had won, regardless of the outcome. He came back from a crushing failure on the vault and proved to himself that he could execute beyond failure. And as it turns out, in one of the most dramatic comebacks in all of sports, he won the gold medal in the men's all-around by 0.012 points, becoming the first U.S. man to ever win the Olympic title. Talk about finishing strong.

BELIEF

The will to do springs from the
knowledge that we can do.

—James Allen

To accomplish great things, we
must not only act, but also dream;
not only plan, but also believe.

—Anatole France

You'll see it when you believe it.

—Dr. Wayne Dyer

A SPIRIT FORGED IN STEEL

On June 23, 1940, Wilma Glodean Rudolph was born prematurely and weighed only 4.5 pounds. Wilma became the twentieth member of a twenty-two-child family of Ed and Blanche Rudolph. The Rudolph's were African Americans living in a time of segregation. Since the local hospital was for whites only and the Rudolphs had little money, Mrs. Rudolph was forced to care for Wilma herself. Wilma's early years were very rough. Her mother nursed her through one illness after another—measles, mumps, scarlet fever, chicken pox, and double pneumonia. A few years after her birth, they discovered that Wilma's left leg and foot were not developing normally and were becoming deformed. The doctors told Mrs. Rudolph that Wilma had polio, she would never walk, and she would have to wear steel braces on her legs. Mrs. Rudolph refused to accept this diagnosis and set out to find a cure. She discovered that Wilma could receive treatment at Meharry Medical College in Nashville. For the next two years, Mrs. Rudolph drove Wilma fifty miles each way to get physical therapy. Eventually, the hospital staff taught Mrs. Rudolph how to do the physical therapy at home. Everyone in the family worked with Wilma, providing her with encouragement to be strong and to get better. Thanks to patience, support, effort, and love from her family, at the age of twelve, Wilma could walk normally without the assistance of crutches, braces, or corrective shoes. She had spent a great deal of her life limited by her illnesses. Wilma felt a freedom that she had never felt. It was then that she decided to become an athlete.

Wilma chose first to pursue basketball just as her older sister did. For three years, she rode the bench, not playing a single game. But Wilma's spirit was forged from steel, and she continued to practice hard, refusing to give

> My mother taught me very early to believe I could achieve any accomplishment I wanted to. The first was to walk without braces.
>
> —Wilma Rudolph

up. In her sophomore year, she became the starting guard for the team and subsequently led the team to a state championship. But Wilma's first love was to run. At the age of sixteen (barely four years free of braces), she participated in the 1956 Olympics in track. She won a bronze medal in the 4 x 100 m relay. However, it was at the state basketball tournament that she was first spotted by Ed Temple, the coach for the women's track team at Tennessee State University. Ed recruited Wilma on a track scholarship and changed the course of her athletic pursuits.

Wilma's most famous athletic achievement was realized at the 1960 Rome Olympics. The little girl who could hardly walk without the assistance of crutches or braces had overcome her challenges and became the first American woman to win three gold medals in a single Olympics.

FOLLOW THE SUN

Ben was nine years old when his father committed suicide in front of him. It was a horrible thing for a father to do to a son, and it had a deep impact on that little boy. Ben would turn to golf as a way to escape the horrors of his childhood. He was a caddie at a local course in Fort Worth, Texas, where he hit balls after work until dark. Golf was the perfect game for him, as it did not require interaction with anyone. Ben loved the game, and he especially loved the way it felt when he perfectly executed a golf shot. Some days, he would hit so many golf balls that his hands would bleed.

At the age of seventeen, Ben set his sights on perfecting the game he loved so much and wanted to join the professional tour. He failed to make it on the tour and was forced to take a full-time job. He continued to practice with the belief that he had what it took to be a great golfer.

A few years later, Ben made another attempt on the tour. In the process, he met his future wife, Valerie. Valerie was an instant inspiration to Ben, and she traveled with him from tournament to tournament. In those days, the professional golf tour schedule was coordinated with the places in the country where the sun stayed out the longest. The players would "follow the sun" as they traveled from one week to the next.

During these early years, Ben struggled to make a living. At one point, he was forced to give up the game for a job with steady income. However, he continued to practice, and with the encouragement of his wife, he returned to the tour for a third try. In 1940, eleven years after turning pro, Ben Hogan won his first professional tournament. For the next four years, he had modest success on the PGA Tour. However, he had an intense focus and concentration on and off the course. This demeanor projected a cold and unfriendly personality. In fact, it was common for him to walk from shot to shot with his head down, staring at his shoe laces. When he did look up, Ben's steely gray eyes and cold stare instantly intimidated anyone who caught his glance. Ultimately, this look would earn him the nickname "the Hawk" and the reputation for being an ice-cold and fierce competitor.

In 1943, just as Ben was beginning to achieve success on the tour, he decided to serve his country, and he joined the U.S. Air Force. During his service, Ben was limited in how much golf he could play. He read news articles about the great success of his fellow competitor Byron Nelson. Nelson dominated the PGA Tour during the time Ben served in World War II. Nelson's record of eighteen wins in one year still stands today and will likely never be broken. At the time, the press anointed Nelson as "Mr. Golf" and "Lord Byron." Ben was both frustrated and motivated by Nelson's success and notoriety. He returned to golf in 1945, determined to establish himself as the dominant player in the game. And he did. For the next three years, Ben dominated the sport by winning thirty-one events, two PGA championships, and the U.S. Open.

In 1949, Ben and Valerie were taking a break from the tour. Driving back to Texas, they ran into a dense fog that forced Ben to slow down to less than ten miles per hour. In a split second, a bus pulled out to pass a truck and was in the direct path of the Hogans' car. In a selfless act, Ben threw himself in front of Valerie to protect her from the impact. The bus hit them head-on, sending the engine into the driver's seat and the steering column into the back seat. Ben would have been killed instantly if he had not tried to protect Valerie. Because of his unselfish courage, Valerie suffered only minor injuries. However, the crash was devastating for Ben and left him clinging to life. He fractured his pelvis, collarbone, and left ankle. Blood clots threatened his life and forced the doctors to limit his blood circulation

by tying off principal veins in his legs. The doctors said it was unlikely he would ever walk again, let alone play professional golf. But Ben was a fierce competitor in sport and life. He was determined to overcome the challenges confronting him, and with great perseverance and the support of his wife, Ben recovered. He gained enough strength to return to golf in 1950, just eleven months after the accident.

In his first tournament back, he forced a playoff with Sam Snead—an amazing accomplishment alone. However, Ben's physical condition caused him to fade in the playoff and ultimately lose to Snead. Even so, this small success proved to Ben that he could compete. He continued to practice hard. Today, Ben Hogan is credited with being the first professional golfer to actually practice. When asked about this, he replied, "You hear stories about me beating my brains out practicing, but...I was enjoying myself. I couldn't wait to get up in the morning so I could hit balls... When I'm hitting the ball where I want, hard and crisply...it's a joy that very few people experience." Five months later, he would win the U.S. Open, reinforcing his belief in himself.

After the accident, Ben's legs were never the same. He could hardly walk eighteen holes without collapsing. Due to this poor condition, he could only play seven tournaments each year. However, for the next three years, Ben Hogan dominated every tournament he entered. He won thirteen of the tournaments he entered, including six majors. In 1953, he only entered six tournaments but won five of them, including three majors. Winning three majors in a single year was a record that would stand for almost fifty years until 2000, when Tiger Woods accomplished the same feat.

Ben Hogan would ultimately retire with sixty-four professional victories and nine major titles, six of which came after the car crash. He is known today as the father of the modern golf swing, and Tiger Woods and Jack Nicklaus consider him to be the best ball striker the game has ever seen.

One of his greatest contributions to the game is the concept of practice. Before Ben Hogan, the idea of practicing the game of golf did not exist. His work ethic and commitment to improvement is the model for today's touring professional.

Ben Hogan overcame a dark childhood memory, early failure at the game of golf, and a debilitating car crash to become one of the legends of the game. He continued to be an ambassador of the game and charitable organizations long after his retirement. Throughout his life, there were many reasons for Ben Hogan to have simply been finished. Instead, he chose to persevere, to fight, and to ultimately Finish Strong.

BELIEVE IN MIRACLES

It was 1980, and the U.S. economy was in a recession. Iranian militants had taken American diplomats and citizens hostage, and Soviet forces had invaded Afghanistan. With the Cold War in full force, President Carter threatened to boycott the Summer Olympics in Moscow in protest of the USSR's actions in Afghanistan. Across America, the events of the time were driving American pride and morale to an all-time low point in history. But a hockey game was about to change all that.

In the 1980 Winter Olympics at Lake Placid, New York, the U.S. hockey team was represented by a collection of young college kids, some with pro hockey aspirations. Under the guidance of their coach, Herb

Brooks, the young American athletes became a fast, well-conditioned, and cohesive team. While some viewed Brooks's coaching methods as somewhat questionable, they did result in the development of a physically and mentally tough young hockey team.

Brooks knew how dangerous his team could be. He also knew that many of their competitors were underestimating his team's potential and had mostly written them off as a medal contender. Brooks would use this miscalculation to his team's advantage.

To make it to the medal round, the U.S. team had to fight hard in each match. In the opening game against Sweden, they scored with twenty-seven seconds remaining to force a 2–2 tie. This was a significant event for the U.S. team, because American Olympic teams had not beaten Swedish teams since 1960. The tie lifted the team's morale and planted that first seed of belief. Next, the American team dominated a strong Czechoslovakian team by winning 7–3, with seven different American players scoring. Again, this was another significant event for the young team to take and build upon, because the Czechoslovakian team was largely believed to be a lock for the silver medal. The U.S. team continued their way through the bracket by winning their next three games, ultimately positioning them for the first medal round against the Soviet team. Belief had turned into passion for the American players.

The young U.S. team had been given essentially no chance to beat the stronger Soviet team. The Soviets had dominated Olympic hockey for years, and their players were considered to be professionals by all accounts because of the strength of the European hockey league and the financial backing of the Soviet Union. The Soviets took great pride in their dominance. In fact, just before the start of the Olympics, they crushed the young American team 10–3 in an exhibition match at Madison Square Garden. It was a humiliating loss in front of the American fans, and it seemed clear that the Soviets team was destined for gold.

Fast-forward a few weeks, and the U.S. team found

themselves up against the Soviet team in the first medal round, battling not only for a medal but also for the pride of America. The tensions between the Soviet Union and the United States were very high, and this hockey game took on greater meaning for both nations.

The Soviet team started strong and took a 2–1 lead early in the first period. With the final seconds winding down in the first period, they made a critical mistake. Thinking that the period was almost over, they backed off and began leaving the ice. In fact, there was just enough time for the U.S. team's Mark Johnson to take a rebounded shot with one second left and drill it into the Soviet team's net. The U.S. team had tied the game 2–2. The Soviet team scored quickly again in the second period, and again the American team answered, resulting in a 3–3 tie going into the third period. The Soviet team had thrown everything it had at the American team, and the young players answered at each blow. At this point, the American players no longer believed that they could beat the Soviet team;

they *knew* they could. Midway through the third period, Mike Eruzione, the team captain, caught the puck and fired it past the Soviet goaltender to give the American team a 4–3 lead with ten minutes remaining. The field house erupted, and the energy level went through the roof. Could they actually pull this off? Ten minutes seemed like an eternity. Team USA would need to Finish Strong to hold off the Soviet assault. And the Soviet players fought hard, firing ten shots for every one shot made by the U.S. team. The level of emotion and energy in the rink was beyond anything you could imagine. As the time wound down, the American fans began the chant "U-S-A, U-S-A." This was not about a hockey game. It was about American pride. The well-conditioned U.S. team held off the Soviet team and won. They finished strong in what became known as the Miracle on Ice.

Today, almost thirty years later, most people believe that this unlikely victory resulted in a gold medal for the USA. It did not. The win over the Soviet team put the U.S. team through to the next round, where they later defeated the Finnish team to win the gold. In six of seven games played, the U.S. team had to come back from a deficit to win. They truly embodied the spirit of belief, persistence, and passion. And they definitely finished strong!

Do you believe in miracles?

—Al Michaels, sports broadcaster, in his famous call as time ran out in the game

DON'T STOP BELIEVING

Ray Kroc, the founder of McDonald's, is a great example of how to Finish Strong. Today, every five hours, somewhere around the world, a new McDonald's restaurant opens. However, what's amazing about McDonald's is that Ray did not conceive the idea until he was fifty-two years old. By that time, he had already been a struggling paper cup salesman, real estate broker, piano player, and milkshake mixer salesman. Here's what Ray said about that time in his life: "I was fifty-two years old. I had diabetes and incipient arthritis. I had lost my gall bladder and most of my thyroid gland in earlier campaigns, but I was convinced that the best was ahead of me."

He deeply believed that this new restaurant concept was his biggest idea ever. He chose to fully commit himself to making it happen. However, to realize his dream, he would have to mortgage his home and borrow heavily. You have to remember that Ray conceived the idea in a time when the family home-dining experience was very much ingrained in our culture. People did not eat out very often. However, Ray believed if Americans could order good food in a clean place and get it fast, they would come. And of course, he was right.

He truly was the father of fast food.

Most of us at fifty-two years old would find every reason not to take the risk and roll the dice on an untested concept. However, Ray believed in himself and was determined to succeed. Today, because of Ray Kroc living his dream, McDonald's serves more than 69 million customers a day across 120 different countries and employs almost two million people around the world. He was a firm believer in the adage that when you find something that you love to do, you'll never have to work another day of your life. He had a vision and took the risk and finished strong.

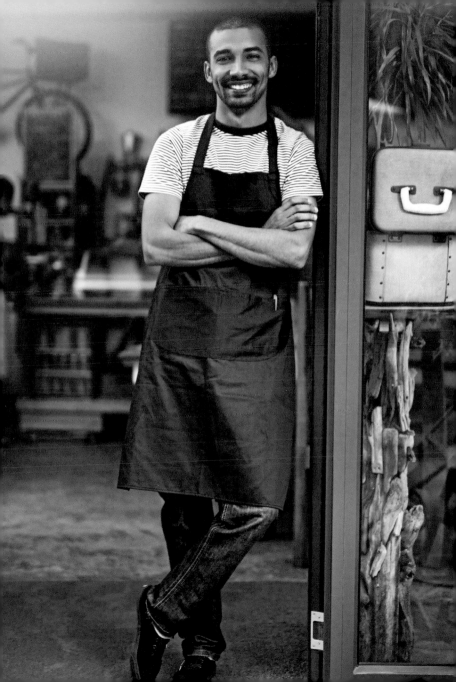

ATTITUDE

Life is 10 percent what you make it and 90 percent how you take it.

—Anonymous

How you respond to the challenge in the second half will determine what you become after the game, whether you are a winner or a loser.

—Lou Holtz

KEEP CLIPPIN' ALONG

By embracing the attitude to Finish Strong, I've created a personal level of accountability that goes with me wherever I go. The first time I really discovered the power of this mindset was early in my selling career. In the early nineties, I sold software systems to commercial banks. A great deal of my selling efforts involved prospecting for leads over the phone. No matter how good you are at selling over the phone, it can be challenging to push yourself to make one more call, and a key to success in selling is making one more call.

As a method of daily goal setting, I started my day in the office by taking twenty-five paper clips from my desktop paper clip holder. I placed the paper clips on a coaster right next to the holder, which was next to the phone.

Each time I engaged in a meaningful selling conversation, I took one of the paper clips from the pile and put it back in the holder. I knew that if I created twenty-five selling conversations each day, my ultimate sales goals would be reached. I made a commitment not to leave the office until every paper clip was put back. There were many times when the day was over for everyone else and I had one paper clip sitting on that coaster, staring at me. To Finish Strong, I needed to have one more selling conversation. I dialed until I succeeded. I never left a paper clip sitting on the coaster, and I never put one back that I did not earn.

The level of activity I created during this time stuffed my sales pipeline with opportunities. My career took off, and I tripled my income in the course of two years, all because I chose to Finish Strong.

The most important thing about goals is having one.

—Geoffrey Abert

TO FINISH FIRST, YOU MUST FIRST FINISH

Because of the success I achieved in sales, I had the good fortune to pursue another passion of mine—motorsports. I had a dream to race at the Indy 500—I like to dream big. Living in Indianapolis at the time, I was overexposed to the world of motorsports. It was intoxicating. So I went to racing school to learn to drive open-wheel race cars. After spending a year racing in the Skip Barber race series, a racing friend of mine (who actually did try to qualify for Indy) took me under his wing. His brother owned a race team in Texas, and I signed up to race one of his Formula Fords in the Sports Car Club of America (SCCA) series. My first race was in October 1993 at Gateway International in

St. Louis, Missouri. When the race started, I was able to hang with the leaders for the first quarter. They were a bit quicker than me, and by the midpoint, they had pulled into a half-lap lead. I became a bit frustrated and began pushing the limits of my car in an effort to catch them. As a result, I pushed my car deep into a corner and lost control, spinning out and losing valuable time. Fortunately, I was able to quickly get back on track, but it seemed unlikely that I could catch the leaders.

I was devastated by my mistake, and winning seemed out of reach.

Sitting in my cockpit speeding down the backstretch with the cars behind quickly catching up, I had a decision to make. Did I get down on myself and coast around the final laps in despair? Or did I pull my belts tight, put my nose down, and set a new realistic goal? I drew upon my commitment to Finish Strong and decided to try to turn the fastest lap of the race. I remember saying out loud, "Come on, Dan. Finish Strong." I took control of my emotions and got going. My vision became clear, everything slowed down around me, and my focus became intense. On the next to final lap, I passed two cars ahead of me. Coming out of the last turn with one lap to go, I could barely see the two leaders at the end of the homestretch, diving into turn one. As I came through turn one, I was shocked to see that the number one and two cars ahead of me had crashed and taken themselves out of the race. I couldn't believe it. Coming out of the last turn, I saw the checkered flag waving. I won! I was shocked. Had I given up after my spin, I would never have caught and passed the two cars in front of me and put myself in a position to win. By choosing to Finish Strong, I ended up winning the first SCCA race I entered. In racing, they say that to finish first, you must first finish. True, but finishing strong is even better.

Success seems to be connected with action. Successful people keep moving. They make mistakes, but they don't quit.

—Conrad Hilton

COMMITMENT

Don't be afraid to take a big step
if one is indicated. You can't cross
a chasm in two small jumps.

—David Lloyd George

The difference between involvement and
commitment is like ham and eggs. The
chicken is involved; the pig is committed.

—Martina Navratilova

Keep on going, and the chances are
that you will stumble on something,
perhaps when you are least expecting
it. I have never heard of anyone
stumbling on something sitting down.

—Charles Kettering

FOCUS ON PRIORITIES

Through the years, choosing to Finish Strong has provided me with many benefits: reaching goals, winning a race, and gaining satisfaction from knowing I gave it my all. By drawing upon my commitment, I have begun learning to enjoy the ride of life. However, one of the greatest benefits that I've received from this mindset involves my family. A great example of how this attitude has helped me relates to my relationship with my two daughters. A regular part of our nighttime routine is to read a story and say our prayers. Sometimes, of course, I'm worn out from my day's work, or I'm thinking about other things that need to be done. In these times, it can be tempting to try to skip the ritual with my daughters,

but I know this would be a mistake. I remind myself of my commitment to Finish Strong and to focus on my true priorities in life. Because as the quote says, "To the world, you may be just one person, but to one person, you may be the world."

The cost of regret far exceeds the price of discipline.

DYING TO MAKE A DIFFERENCE

After a two-year battle with cancer, teenager Miles Levin unfortunately lost his fight. However, during his final years, he achieved a level of self-awareness, courage, and wisdom that most of us will never reach. Miles chose to post his observations on a carepages.com blog, and through his writings, he inspired thousands of people. He wrote with amazing grace and eloquence.

Some of his posts were short: *"Dying is not what scares me. It's dying having no impact."* Some were long and philosophical. But each post served a significant purpose in that it challenged the reader to think more deeply about life, death, and making a difference. Through his expressions, Miles left this world a better place than when he came into it. I can only hope that I do the same with my life. Here's what Miles said just one month after being diagnosed with terminal cancer:

I WENT TO THE DRIVING RANGE the other day and I was thinking…I was thinking how you start out with a big bucket full of golf balls, and you just start hitting away carelessly. You have dozens of them, each individual ball means nothing to you so just hit, hit, hit. One ball gone is practically inconsequential when subtracted from your bottomless bucket. There are no practice swings or technique re-evaluations after a bad shot, because so many more tries remain. Yet eventually you start to have to reach down toward the bottom of the bucket to scavenge for another shot and you realize that tries are running out. Now with just a handful left, each swing becomes more meaningful. The right technique becomes more crucial, so between each shot you take a couple practice swings and a few deep breaths.

There is a very strong need to end on a good note, even if every preceding shot was terrible, getting it right at the end means a lot. You know as you tee up your last ball, "This is my final shot, I want to crush this with perfection; I must make this count."

Like Miles suggested, we should treat each day as a precious ball of life. Take your time, take a breath, and make a practice swing. Make each shot count, and most of all, Finish Strong!

Limited quantities or limited time brings a new, precious value and significance to anything you do. Live every day shooting as if it's your last shot. I know I have to.

—Miles Levin

I have tried my best to show what it is to persevere, and what it means to be strong.

—Miles Levin

OVERNIGHT SUCCESS

Finishing Strong in life, sport, or business does not always involve overcoming a challenge in a moment in time. When you live the attitude, it becomes part of you and part of your life. In some cases, you will find strength to Finish Strong in a blink of an eye. For example, you may get an extra burst of energy to finish the last repetition in an exercise. Other times, it will fuel you through a project that may take months. However, sometimes it can take a lifetime to realize the benefits of your commitment to Finish Strong. A man named William is testimony to this.

"Harriet Beecher Stowe praised him in the pages of *Uncle Tom's Cabin*," writes historian and biographer Kevin Belmonte.

"Novelist E. M. Forster compared him to Gandhi. Abraham Lincoln invoked his memory in a celebrated speech. In the houses of Parliament, Nelson Mandela recalled his tireless labors on behalf of the sons and daughters of Africa, calling Britain 'the land of William Wilberforce—who dared to stand up to demand that the slaves in our country should be freed.'"

It was in 1787 that William Wilberforce first became leader of the parliamentary campaign of the Committee for the Abolition of the Slave Trade. In May 1789, he made his first major speech on the subject of abolition in the House of Commons. However, getting people to listen was only a small first step. In April 1791, Wilberforce introduced the first parliamentary bill to abolish the slave trade, which was easily defeated by 163 votes to 88. Six subsequent attempts to pass the bill also failed, the last in 1805. Like any great leader, Wilberforce had cast his vision clearly and often, but the outcome had not yet been reached. Still, he persisted.

Two years later, the bill came before Parliament

again with a different result. In March 1807, the Slave Trade Act was passed, abolishing the slave trade from the British Empire.

It was a momentous victory yet not the ultimate objective that Wilberforce sought. He continued his campaign for the emancipation of all slaves. Finally, on July 26, 1833, over forty-five years after setting out, Wilberforce received news that the bill for the abolition of slavery had passed its third reading in the House of Commons. He died three days later, but the momentum he created saw his vision through. One month after his death, Parliament passed the Slavery Abolition Act, giving all slaves in the British Empire their freedom.

Have the dogged determination to follow through to achieve your goal, regardless of circumstances or whatever other people say, think, or do.

—Paul J. Meyer

PURPOSE

**Nothing changes
until something moves.**

—Unknown

**It doesn't matter where you came from.
It only matters where you are going.**

—Brian Tracy

**The secret to success is
constancy to purpose.**

—Benjamin Disraeli

REDEFINE YOUR LIMITS

ABC Sports called it one of the most defining moments in sports. After leading the 1982 Ironman Triathlon in Kona, Hawaii, for more than seven hours, Julie Moss collapsed fifty feet from the finish line. Millions of television viewers painfully watched Julie stagger and fall, stagger and fall, then stagger and crawl across the finish line. What they did not see was the mental transformation that took place within Julie during that time. This was a defining moment in her life.

Julie was a twenty-three-year-old student participating in her first triathlon, largely to do research for her exercise physiology thesis. She entered the event because she believed it would provide her with valuable experience to incorporate into her thesis. She did not consider herself to be an exceptional athlete and later explained, "I used to dread getting called onto the court for volleyball or having to serve in tennis," she says of her high school sporting days. "I really wasn't ready for the pressure of leading the race."

But leading an Ironman race can have a powerful effect on people, and Julie experienced that firsthand. During the midpoint of the run portion—the final leg—her desire to simply finish began to evolve into a desire to finish fast and finish first. Never in her entire life had she experienced that competitive side to her psyche. However, she was about to experience the effects of her poor diet and hydration during the race. At that time, very little was understood about nutrition, hydration, and high-performance activity. The PowerBar hadn't been invented yet, and most athletes believed that bananas and water were the nutritional staples of high performance; we know different today. Julie began to feel weak and her body began to shut

down. With about seven miles to go, she was forced to add intervals of walking, then running. Her body was shutting down, but her mind was not. "It took all my focus just to keep my body working," she recalled. "The image was that I was pretty out of it, but it was taking all my focus just to keep going. I had to concentrate so much on how I placed my foot on the ground. If I was off by a bit, my leg would just buckle."

With one hundred yards to go, Julie's mind began to play tricks on her. She imagined herself running across the finish line and kept trying to run instead of walk to the finish. Later, she said that she probably would have won the race if she simply decided to walk instead of run. So for the last fifty yards, she continued to fall, rise, step, and fall, over and over again. It was painful to watch. Julie was on her hands and knees within feet of the finish line when the second-place runner passed Julie to win the race. A few seconds later, Julie crawled across the finish line, creating one of the most dramatic finishes in sports history. For Julie, it was much more than a generic defining moment in sports; this was her defining moment.

Everyone has a defining moment at some point in their life. Julie's just happened to be captured on film and in front of millions of people. She tapped an inner strength she never knew she possessed and rose above the physical and mental adversity confronting her to achieve her goal. For Julie, this moment in time shifted the course of her life by redefining her physical and mental personal limits.

Heavyweight Champion Jim Braddock preparing for his fight against Joe Louis, t the hotel Golfmore on June 18, 1937 in Grand Beach, MI.
Photo by The Stanley Weston Archive/Getty Images

CAPITALIZE ON CATASTROPHE

The story of Jim J. Braddock, the "Cinderella Man," is one of my favorites. It's about a working man's rise to the top, his fall to the very bottom, and then his ascension to heights he never imagined. And through it all, he discovered the true meaning of life.

Jim Braddock spent the better part of the 1920s boxing in the light heavyweight division. He gained a reputation for being a fierce competitor with a right-hand punch that could stop a bulldozer. His rise through the professional ranks began in 1926. He won most of his fights and earned a respectable reputation and living. By all accounts, Jim was a successful man with a good life.

Jim's first big shot came on a warm summer night in 1929. He faced Tommy Loughran for the light heavyweight championship of the world. Loughran was a young and bright fighter who knew how dangerous Jim's right hand could be. He studied Jim's style and went into the fight with a strategy to avoid the right hand. His research paid off, and Jim was never able to land a solid punch with his right. The fight went fifteen rounds, and Jim lost the decision to Loughran.

Jim took this loss very hard. Everything he had worked to achieve seemed to be gone. But little did he know how much harder things would get. Less than two months after the loss to Loughran on September 3, 1929, the stock market crashed and thrust America into the Great Depression.

Like millions of Americans, Jim Braddock lost everything in the crash. With no work available, he continued to box to provide for his family. Unfortunately, Jim's boxing career hit the skids during this time. He lost sixteen of twenty-two fights. To make matters worse, he shattered his powerful right hand and lost his greatest boxing asset. Under pressure to support his family, Jim quit boxing and filed for government relief. For the next few years, Jim struggled to make ends meet. He worked odd jobs on the docks and took whatever other work he could find. His family finances grew worse, and at times, they had very little food or heat for their apartment. It was during these years that Jim Braddock discovered how important his family was to him. Because of this emotional time in his life, Jim rediscovered the true meaning of winning.

A favorite saying of mine is that "God's timing is never early and never late." This was true for Jim Braddock in 1934. Due to a last-minute cancellation and the dogged determination of his manager, Jim was given the opportunity to fight on the undercard for the heavyweight championship bout between Max Baer and Primo Carnera at Madison Square Garden. However, there were compelling reasons for him not to take the fight. For one, the fight was at the heavyweight class, and Jim was not a heavyweight fighter. In fact, he was almost forty pounds lighter than the average heavyweight. Also, his right hand was not the same as before, and he was uncertain if it would hold up under the stress. And finally, he had not been training for the fight. None of this mattered to Jim. To him, this was an opportunity to make some money to improve his family's well-being. As slight a chance as it was, Jim believed he could win, and that meant a better future for his family. Winning now meant so much more than it did before. With no training and a bum right hand, Jim shocked the boxing community by knocking out John Griffin in the third round. Jim later said that his time spent working on the docks had kept him in shape and also helped him to develop a strong left hook, which no one expected.

As word spread of the upset, Jim's popularity grew, and the fight promoters leveraged this popularity to their advantage. As a result, he was given a shot at John Henry Lewis, a fighter who had previously beaten

him. For this fight, Jim was a huge underdog. Yet again, Jim delivered with a tenth-round victory. In doing so, Jim Braddock became an inspiration to the nation during a time that desperately needed something to cheer about. Millions of Americans related to Jim and his working man's story.

In the spring of 1935, Jim was matched up against Art Lasky. Lasky was the number one contender to fight Max Baer, the reigning heavyweight champion. At the time, there were no discussions about Jim getting a shot at Baer, because nobody believed he could beat Lasky. The fight promoters viewed this fight mostly as a way to capitalize on Jim's popularity and make a buck off him—Jim winning just did not seem like an option. Jim took Lasky to fifteen rounds. In doing so, he punished Lasky so much that he won a unanimous decision. With this victory, he became the number one contender to fight Max Baer for the heavyweight championship of the world, less than a year after working on the docks. The Cinderella Man was born.

Jim faced Max Baer on June 13, 1935, at Madison Square Garden. He entered the ring a ten-to-one underdog and gave up over twenty pounds in weight to Baer. Baer was a ferocious fighter with a hammering right hand who had previously killed two other fighters in the ring. Jim learned a valuable lesson from his earlier loss to Tommy Loughran. He studied Baer's fight footage and identified a strategy to avoid Baer's crushing right hand, just as Loughran had done to him. In one of the greatest upsets in all sports history, the Cinderella Man battled Baer for fifteen rounds, winning a unanimous decision to become the heavyweight champion of the world.

In less than a year, Jim Braddock turned his life completely around. Through his personal trials, he was able to redefine the meaning of his life and thus tap an inner strength greater than he ever knew he had. It was this new strength that empowered him to achieve his goals. When presented with the opportunity to make a comeback, the shift he had made mentally prepared him for the fight better than any physical training could have. Jim's new outlook on life lived on past his boxing career, and he went on to lead a successful and prosperous life until his death in 1974.

DISCIPLINE

Great beginnings are not as important as the way one finishes.

—Dr. James Dobson

Nothing will work unless you do.

—John Wooden

What it lies in our power to do, it lies in our power not to do.

—Aristotle

DON'T LET LIFE PIN YOU DOWN

Kyle Maynard is a regular guy with a love of competition. He knows that to truly live, you must set your sights on a goal and never give up. The fire that burns in his belly helped propel him to contend for the Georgia state high school wrestling championship in 2004. Not such a big deal you might say—except for the remarkable fact that Kyle has no arms or legs. He was born a congenital amputee, his arms ending at his elbows, his legs at his knees.

The first time I saw Kyle on an ESPN special (he won an ESPY award for the Best Athlete with a Disability in 2004), I was immediately struck by the confidence that he exhibited, undaunted by his physical limitations.

During the special, they showed Kyle doing all the things that any other person or athlete would do. He spoke with passion and conviction. I was amazed to see him training hard, lifting weights—he has cannon-balls for shoulders. Using a specially designed attach-ment, he was pushing more than double his own body weight. I was instantly inspired to learn more about this amazing person.

From the beginning, Kyle's parents, Anita and Scott, were determined to raise a successful child. They insisted that he learned to feed himself and play with other kids like any other child would. When Kyle saw other kids picking up crayons with their fingers, he learned to pick them up by using the crease in his short but sensitive biceps.

His grandmother Betty was a source of inspiration and often took him to the grocery store, where she would instill a sense of confidence by encouraging Kyle to sit up and look folks in the eye and smile. He was fitted with prosthetic devices at a young age but quickly dismissed them because they were too restrictive. He wanted to be free to run and play just like the other kids, and those devices kept him from doing so.

Kyle led an active childhood. He played street hockey with his friends (he was the goalie), and in sixth grade, he made the football team. Kyle hung tough on the football team, but his physical differences put him at a disadvantage against other players. Eventually, his father encouraged him to try another sport that would put Kyle on an even plane with his competition—wrestling.

Kyle started wrestling in sixth grade. He lost his first thirty-five matches. During this period of time, Kyle had to dig deep to find the confidence to continue. However, he was a warrior, and he didn't like to lose. With the support of his father, a former wrestler, he learned to train with weights, became very strong, and learned some moves unique to his strengths. Kyle overcame the self-doubt he felt during his early wrestling days and became a winner. In his senior year, Kyle won thirty-five times on the varsity squad and qualified for the state championship, where he won his first three matches and had to face his final opponent with a broken nose. Although Kyle did not win the state championship, he gained a level of self-confidence and became a source of inspiration for everyone he met.

Kyle is truly an extraordinary man with great accomplishments. Kyle graduated high school and attended the University of Georgia, where he continued to wrestle and inspire others. He was inducted into the National Wresting Hall of Fame in 2005 and received the

ESPN Espy award for Best Athlete with a Disability. Not to be outdone by his own success, he became the first congenital amputee to climb Mt. Kilimanjaro without prosthetics—a feat that took him ten days to accomplish. Kyle is a professional motivational speaker, but what he has to say has little to do with his perceived physical differences. Rather, he talks of overcoming fear and doubt and what it takes to compete and win, just as any other champion would. Kyle was never pinned by an opponent in his wrestling days. What a fitting metaphor for his life.

It's not what happens to you in life that matters. It's how you choose to respond that does. Always choose to Finish Strong.

—Dan Green

II° série K l m n o p

III° série u v x y z ç e

IV° série â ê î ô û ë ï

; , ? ! ( )

NES IRRÉGULI

APOSTROPHE
OU
ABRÉVIATIF

— | Òou S ae

+ − X .

American university student Helen Keller during a tribute to Louis Braille for the 100th Anniversary of his death at The Sorbonne in June 1952. (Photo by Keystone-France/Gamma-Keystone via Getty Images)

BELIEVING IS SEEING

In stark contrast to many of the athletic endeavors featured in this book, the story of Helen Keller is one that also exemplifies the Finish Strong spirit: overcoming great adversity to achieve success.

Helen was born in 1880 into an affluent Southern family in Alabama. At the age of nineteen months, Helen was stricken ill and left deaf and blind. I can remember when my daughters were that age. They were alive, aware, vibrant, happy, and engaging. Can you imagine the fear that little girl must have felt when her world went dark? In fact, as the years progressed, Helen became wild and hard to control. If it were not for her young friend Martha Washington, the daughter of one of the

Keller family's servants, Helen may have been put into a sanitarium to live out her life in complete darkness. However, Martha befriended Helen and taught her to communicate through sign language. She taught Helen over sixty different signs that helped her communicate with her family. Most of us think of Anne Sullivan as the "miracle worker," when in fact it was young Martha who truly helped Helen's world open up. Experts agree that Martha's help was critical to Helen's later success. It's ironic that because of her limited communication, she became demanding, spoiled, and uncontrollable. When she was six, Helen's mother reached out to friends to find help for Helen. She was referred to a specialist working with deaf children—Alexander Graham Bell. Bell spent time with Helen and ended up referring her to the Perkins Institute for the Blind. And this is where she met Anne Sullivan.

Anne was a twenty-year-old graduate of the school and was partially blind. She had been completely blind, but through a series of operations, she recovered part of her sight. Anne understood Helen's world. She received permission to take Helen away from her family to help her focus. After taking Helen into seclusion and isolating her from her family, she was able to essentially break her of her tantrums and ill behavior. Under Anne's guidance, Helen's world opened up exponentially. Her sight and sound limitations became great strengths and provided her with great wisdom.

Helen went on to become the first blind person to ever graduate from college. She traveled the world as a famous speaker and author. She is remembered as an advocate for people with disabilities amid numerous other causes. In 1915, she founded Helen Keller International, a nonprofit organization for preventing blindness. In 1920, she helped to found the American Civil Liberties Union (ACLU). Helen and Anne Sullivan became very close friends, and they traveled the world together, meeting international dignitaries from more than forty countries. Helen also met some amazing people along her journey. She met every U.S. president from Grover Cleveland to Lyndon B. Johnson and was friends with many famous figures, including Alexander Graham Bell, Charlie Chaplin, and Mark Twain. Helen passed away in 1968 at the age of eighty-seven.

I have to ask, how could a little six-year-old who was deaf and blind in the 1800s rise to such prominence and make such a difference in the world? Without question her mother, Martha Washington, and Anne Sullivan have to be given a great deal of credit. But I believe that the foundation for her success stemmed from within the spirit of Helen herself. Without the deep-seated desire to learn and to rise above the challenges before her, she could not have overcome her physical limitations regardless of how much help she had. At the end of the day, we must all eventually look inward to grow outward. Helen understood this better than most. Like many of the people in this book, in her own way, Helen Keller was a champion who clearly finished strong.

We don't see things as they are;
we see things as we are.

—Anaïs Nin

RISK

Play the game for more than you
can afford to lose...only then
will you learn the game.

—Unknown

People who take risks are the
people you'll lose against.

—John Sculley

Only those who will risk going too far can
possibly find out how far one can go.

—T. S. Eliot

LIFE WITH NO REGRETS

I was a freshman at Oklahoma State in 1983 when the Nebraska Cornhuskers came to town to play our Cowboys. The Cornhuskers had dominated all their opponents so far and were the number one ranked team in college football.

They opened their season by crushing Penn State, the defending national champions, 44–6. Prior to coming to Stillwater, they had outscored their opponents 289 to 56.

I remember the game like it was yesterday, because we gave them their first and only real scare that year, losing 14–10. It was a heartbreaking loss for us. However, it was also very memorable because of the great players I got to see. Mike Rozier went on to win the Heisman

Trophy that year, Turner Gill was an absolute wizard to watch at quarterback, and wide receiver Irving Fryar ultimately became the number one NFL draft pick.

In 1983, the head coach for Nebraska was Tom Osborne. He had never won a national championship and was under tremendous pressure to do so, but by all accounts, he was on his way to bringing Nebraska their first championship. His offense was probably the greatest college offense ever to take the field. They finished their season with a perfect record and entered the Orange Bowl as the number one ranked team in the country.

They faced the Miami Hurricanes. The Hurricanes had entered their season unranked and were slaughtered in their opener by number seven ranked Florida. That was their first and only loss of the season. After that, the Hurricanes dominated every game they played. As a result, they entered the Orange Bowl as the fourth ranked team.

Two key games had been decided prior to the Orange Bowl. The number two ranked Texas Longhorns were upset in the Cotton Bowl by number three ranked Georgia, and the Auburn Tigers put away Michigan in the Sugar Bowl. Because of these events, the Orange Bowl would be played for the national title.

As you can imagine, the game was hyped by the media as the game of the century. Could the previously unknown Hurricanes actually win? Would Tom Osborne get his first national title? Could the Nebraska offense be stopped? The game lived up to the hype. It was an emotional roller coaster to watch and would take too many pages to fully recap. But the simple truth is this:

with 1:46 left to play in the game, the Cornhuskers had the ball on Miami's twenty-six-yard line with fourth down and eight to go. They were trailing Miami 31–24. In one of the greatest plays in college football history, Turner Gill ran the option to the right, then pitched the ball to Jeff Smith, who ran it in for a touchdown and pulled the Cornhuskers within one point with under a minute left to play. They could tie the game with an extra point, or they could win outright with a two-point conversion. Since there was no overtime to decide an outright winner, a tied game would leave the championship to be decided by the coaches and media polls. But an outright win would seal the championship for the Huskers.

What happened next perfectly defines the meaning

Nobody who ever gave his best regretted it!

—George Halas

of risk. Tom Osborne put the championship on the line and went for two points and the win. He had the best run offense in the country and was completely confident that they could pull it off. He also knew that Miami would be expecting the run. So instead of using his bread-and-butter run offense, he opted to pass the ball. Gill's pass fell incomplete, and after a failed onside kick attempt, Nebraska lost their first game of the year and the national championship.

The next morning, football fans across the country debated the "go for two" call. Many argued that given a tie, Nebraska would have easily won the vote for the title. Osborne and his team had a different perspective. They wanted to Finish Strong and win the game and the championship outright. They took the path they believed would get them there. It was a calculated risk that Osborne never second-guessed. In this instance, it didn't work, but they gave it their best shot, and to this day, he does not regret it.

BEGINNINGS

This is the last chapter in my book, and I'll bet that you've noticed an emerging theme throughout. For most of the champions, their great accomplishment was not the end of their greatness; rather it was the beginning of greater things to come. Each used their moment in time to propel them forward in life.

Bethany Hamilton survived the shark attack to become a world-class surfer and an inspiration to thousands of people around the world. After he achieved his success in boxing, Jim Braddock repaid the government aid money that he was given during his hard times and went on to live a full and prosperous life. John Baker's commitment to give his best effort lives on at the elementary school bearing his name. After her Olympic glory, Wilma Rudolph championed civil rights causes and inspired thousands of children as a teacher. Ray Kroc's belief in himself ultimately led to the creation of the Ronald McDonald House charity, a place dedicated to helping cancer victims and their families find peace during difficult times.

The Finish Strong attitude is grounded in the principle that you never "get there" in life and that you should always keep moving forward. I love the way that John Naber, the four-time gold medal–winning Olympic swimming champion, characterizes his achievement. When asked if winning four Olympic gold medals was the highlight of his life, he replied, "I hope not. I've still got a lot of living left to do, and I hope that my greatest achievement is still in front of me."

May your greatest achievements be in front of you, and may you always **Finish Strong**.

Effort only fully releases its reward after a person refuses to quit.

—Napoleon Hill

ABOUT THE AUTHOR

Dan is an entrepreneur with a passion for finishing strong in everything he does. Over the past thirty years, he has excelled in his roles as salesman, sales leader, sales trainer, patented inventor, race car driver, author, speaker, husband, and father. Adopting the Finish Strong attitude has been a driving force in Dan's life and a key catalyst in achieving his goals in business, sports, and life. Dan was the cofounder of the inspirational book publisher Simple Truths and also the cofounder of Inspire Kindness, a

social do-good brand that inspires individuals to use kindness in their lives to inspire others.

Dan is the author of three inspirational books: *Finish Strong*, *Finish Strong Teen Athlete*, and *Finish Strong Motivational Quotes*. Collectively, his books have been purchased by more than 250,000 people across the globe.

Since receiving the trademark rights to the words *Finish Strong* in 1996, Dan has been the evangelist for incorporating its message of challenge and inspiration in every aspect of life. During this time, thousands of people from all walks of life have adopted the Finish Strong attitude in their lives, ultimately beating the odds to overcome adversity and achieve their dreams.

In 2009, Drew Brees, the quarterback for the New Orleans Saints, purchased a copy of *Finish Strong* and gave it to every member of the team. Finish Strong became their battle cry on the way to the team's first ever national football world title. Dan partnered with the Brees Dream Foundation in 2009 to create a Finish

Strong T-shirt to raise money for the charity. More than sixty thousand shirts were sold in less than seven days and over $300,000 was raised for charity.

For more information about Dan, to inquire about speaking engagements, or to learn more about incorporating Finish Strong into your next event, you can send your request to Dan at contact@finishstrong.live.

I have fought a good fight, I have finished the race, I have kept the faith.

—2 Timothy 4:7

NEW! Only from Simple Truths®

IGNITE READS
spark impact in just one hour

IGNITE READS IS A NEW SERIES OF 1-HOUR READS WRITTEN BY WORLD-RENOWNED EXPERTS!

These captivating books will help you become the best version of yourself, allowing for new opportunities in your personal and professional life. Accelerate your career and expand your knowledge with these powerful books written on today's hottest ideas.

TRENDING BUSINESS AND PERSONAL GROWTH TOPICS

Read in an hour or less

Leading experts and authors

Bold design and captivating content

EXCLUSIVELY AVAILABLE ON SIMPLETRUTHS.COM

Need a training framework?
Engage your team with discussion guides and PowerPoints for training events or meetings.

Want your own branded editions?
Express gratitude, appreciation, and instill positive perceptions to staff or clients by adding your organization's logo to your edition of the book.

Add a supplemental visual experience
to any meeting, training, or event.

Contact us for special corporate discounts!
(800) 900-3427 x247 or
simpletruths@sourcebooks.com

LOVED WHAT YOU READ AND WANT MORE?

Sign up today and be the FIRST to receive advance copies of Simple Truths® NEW releases written and signed by expert authors. Enjoy a complete package of supplemental materials that can help you host or lead a successful event. This high-value program will uplift you to be the best version of yourself!

— SIMPLE TRUTHS —
ELITE CLUB
ONE MONTH. ONE BOOK. ONE HOUR.

Your monthly dose of motivation, inspiration, and personal growth.